Take the Next Step™

KOOLER DESIGN STUDIO inc.

Designs by Rona Horn

Annie's Attic®

Introduction

As you look through *Take the Next Step*, you will see beautiful designs that include a wide variety of materials, including: glass beads made by several different artists; silver, copper and brass wire; linen and cotton cord; and silk string. There are also chains, charms, buttons, scrapbooking materials, as well as stone and resin beads. These jewelry designs offer an opportunity to try different techniques such as stringing, basic wire techniques and simple macramé. There are designs that are simply strung, but have additional fibers added, some are put together simply by opening and closing jump rings or chain links, but the eye-catching components make them look much more complicated. Applying these ideas to your own designs will enable you to make wonderful jewelry no matter what your skill level or previous experience.

All the projects in this book are beginner, easy or intermediate and offer choices for all skill levels, while still helping you build the skills to make anything in this book. Beginners and experienced jewelry makers alike will find new ideas and new ways to apply what they know. Since skill levels can vary from publication to publication, here is how we define them for this book:

Beginner: No previous skills needed, usually includes one very basic technique, sometimes two.

Easy: Basic techniques only or mixing two or three basic techniques.

Intermediate: Requires some comfort with jewelry making. The instructions may mix several techniques, or may have just a few techniques, but require working with multiple parts or strands at the same time.

So select a design, gather your tools and materials and get ready to *Take the Next Step* in jewelry making.

Meet the Designer

Rona Horn's lifelong interest in color and texture has led her through many different crafts from knitting, needlework and beading to creating her own glass beads. Rona discovered the joys of lampworking and jewelry almost 10 years ago and soon after began Rona Horn Designs, offering her beads and jewelry online, and in local gift shops and bead stores. Rona is co-founder of Imagine Global, an organization providing a market for handcrafted items from women in impoverished countries in

Central Asia. She is also co-owner of Imagine Together, offering kits, supplies and tools for needle felting and wet felting. Rona has taught classes on a wide variety of techniques and using many different materials. She is co-author of *The Big Book of Needle Felting*, and her designs and articles have appeared in several national publications. Rona currently resides in Eau Claire, Wis., with her husband, Gary, her two daughters, Kayleigh and Bethany, and an ever-changing variety of household pets.

Contents

Visual Glossary

Tools

Crimping Pliers are for just what their name implies—crimping! The back slot puts a seam in the middle of the crimp tube, separating the ends of the flex wire and trapping it firmly. The front slot rounds out the tube and turns it into a small, tidy bead.

Chain-Nose Pliers are the most useful tool in your entire toolbox. They are used for holding, opening and closing jump rings and bending sharp angles.

Round-Nose Pliers are intended for turning round loops. They do not work well for holding or grasping since they tend to leave a small dent.

Flat-Nose Pliers are a wire power tool. They are excellent for turning sharp corners, holding items and for opening and closing jump rings.

Wire Flush Cutters leave one flat side and one pointed side on each cut. Using flush cutters is especially important when working with heavy gauges of wire (20-gauge or smaller). One side of the cutter is flat and the other is indented.

Memory Wire Shears Because memory wire is harder than beading wire or craft wire, it will damage regular wire nippers or scissors. These heavy-duty shears easily cut through memory wire and leave a clean end.

Nylon-Jaw Pliers can be used to harden or straighten wire.

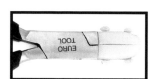

Jeweler's Hammers have fine, smooth curved heads to leave a clean impression. The round peen side works well for texturing wire and metal sheet.

A Bench Block is a flat, smooth piece of hardened steel. Hammering on top of a block flattens out and hardens the wire. Bench blocks are also used for stamping metal to get a clean impression.

Materials

Eye Pins are wires with a loop on one end and a straight portion of wire where beads can be strung. Length and gauges vary; most earrings use 24-gauge eye pins from 1½–2½ inches.

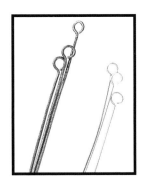

Head Pins are a piece of wire with a stop end like a fine nail head. A bead slides onto the head pin and stops on the head. Lengths and gauges vary; most earrings use 24-gauge head pins from 1½–2½ inches.

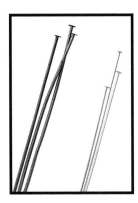

Jump Rings are one of the most versatile findings used in jewelry making. They come in all sizes, gauges and metals. They are measured by diameter (width) and gauge (weight).

Ear Wires come in many different styles. Regular fishhook styles are the most common and the easiest to make yourself. Recommended weight for ear wires is either 22- or 20-gauge.

Crimp Tubes are small soft metal cylinders that can be flattened or formed around flexible beading wire to secure the ends. They are an essential component for bead-stringing projects.

Wire comes in many sizes or *gauges*. Gauge is the measured diameter of the wire. The higher the number, the thinner the wire. Wire can be tempered soft, half-hard or hard, which refers to its stiffness. Copper, silver and gold-filled are most commonly used for jewelry.

Flexible Beading Wire comes in several weights from .010–.026-inch-diameter and is designed for stringing. It is available in precious metal and several colors and is made from 7 to 49 strands of steel wire, twisted and encased in a flexible plastic coating. Ends are finished with crimp beads using either crimping or chain-nose pliers.

Basics Step by Step

Creating your own beaded jewelry is easy and only takes a few tools. Practice these techniques using less expensive metal findings. Once your finishing techniques are perfected, use real sterling silver or vermeil (real gold plating over sterling silver) to add elegance to your beadwork.

Opening & Closing Jump Rings

Jump rings are one of the most versatile findings used in jewelry making. They come in all sizes and gauges.

Use two pairs of smooth chain-nose pliers (bent or flat-nose pliers work fine as a second plier). (Photo A)

Photo A

Push ring open with right plier while holding across the ring with left plier. To close, hold in the same way and rock the ring back and forth until ring ends rub against each other or you hear a click. Moving the ring past closed then back hardens the ring and assures a tight closure. (Photo B)

Photo B

Making an Eye Pin or Round Loop

Eye pins should be made with half-hard wire to make sure they hold their shape. 22-gauge will fit through most beads, with the exception of many semi-precious stones. Most Czech glass beads and 4mm crystals will fit on 20-gauge wire.

The length used for the eye loop depends on how big you want the loop. Here we will use ⅜ inch for a moderate size loop.

Flush trim end of wire. (Photo A)

Photo A

Photo B

Using chain-nose pliers, make a 90-degree bend ⅜ inch from end of wire. (Photo B)

Using round-nose pliers, grasp the end of the wire so no wire sticks out between plier blades. (Photo C1)

Begin making a loop by rolling your hand away from your body. Don't try to make the entire loop in one movement. Roll your hand ¼ turn counterclockwise. (Photo C2)

Photo C1

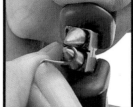

Photo C2

Without removing pliers from loop, open plier blade slightly and pivot plier back toward your body clockwise about ¼ turn. (Photo D)

Photo D

Photo E

Close plier onto the wire and roll the loop until it comes around, next to the 90-degree bend. (Photo E)

Open and close eye-pin loops the same way as jump rings by pushing open front to back. (Photo F)

Photo F

Making Wire-Wrapped Loops

Practice wire wrapping with either 22- or 24-gauge wire. Harden slightly by pulling on one end with the other end clamped in a vise, or pull one or two times through nylon-jaw pliers. (Photo A)

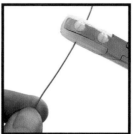

Photo A

Photo B

Make a 90-degree bend about 1½ inches from end of the wire using chain-nose pliers. (Photo B)

Using round-nose pliers, grab wire about ⅜ inch away from the 90-degree bend and roll your hand away from yourself, toward the bend, until a loop is halfway formed. (Photos C1 and C2)

Photo C1

Photo C2

Without removing plier from forming loop, open the jaw and rotate plier clockwise about ¼ turn. (Photo D)

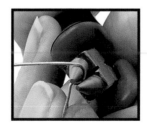

Photo D

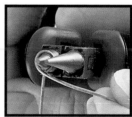

Photo E

Grab the end of the wire with your left (non-dominant) hand and pull it around the rest of the way until it crosses itself and completes the loop. (Photo E)

Switch to chain-nose pliers, holding across the loop. Wrap tail around wire under loop with your left hand. If you are using a heavy gauge of wire, it is often easier to use a second plier to pull the tail around instead of your fingers. (Photos F1 and F2)

Photo F1   **Photo F2**

Flush cut wire as close to the wrap as possible. Tuck end down if needed, using chain-nose pliers. (Photos G1 and G2)

Photo G1   **Photo G2**

To create a wrap on the opposite end of the bead, leave a gap equal to wrap space on first end. Grasp to the right of the wrap space and make a 90-degree bend. (Photos H1 and H2)

Photo H1   **Photo H2**

Repeat from Photo C–H to complete.

Hammering Wire

Hammering hardens and flattens round wire. This can be especially important when making ear wires or clasps that need to hold their shape. Always use a smooth, hardened steel surface to guarantee a clean finish. Any marks or scars on a bench block or hammer will impress on the surface of wire or sheet metal.

Create your shape from wire. Keep hammer flat to prevent marring wire. Flip over after a few taps and hammer on opposite side. Don't get carried away; if you hammer too much, metal becomes brittle and breaks. (Photo A)

Photo A

Crimping

String a crimp bead onto flexible wire. String clasp or ring and pass tail of flexible wire back through crimp to form a loop.

Hold wires parallel and make sure crimp is positioned correctly. Using front slot on plier, shape crimp into a small oval. (Photo A)

Photo A

Put oval into back slot of plier and squeeze to make fold in the center with one wire on each side of fold. (Photo B)

Photo B

Return to front slot and squeeze again to tighten crimp. Do a few more rotations and squeezes to solidify and shape crimp bead. Trim wire tail. (Photo C)

Photo C

Knots

Overhand Knot Make a loop and pass the cord behind the loop, over the front cord. Pull to tighten.

Overhand Knot

Square Knot Make one overhand knot, passing the right cord over the left. Repeat overhand knot, this time passing left end over right. Pull to tighten.

Square Knot

Lark's Head Knot Fold stringing material in half and pass the folded end through the loop through which you are attaching cord. Pull ends of cord through the loop made at the fold to tighten.

Lark's Head Knot

Half-Hitch Knot Use at least two lines, a core line and a working line. Cross working line over core line creating a figure "4". Bring working line tail under core line and up through loop of figure "4". Pull tight, repeat. After multiple knots have been made, knots will twist around core line

Half-Hitch Knot

Metric Conversion Charts

METRIC CONVERSIONS

yards	x	.9144	=	metres (m)
yards	x	91.44	=	centimetres (cm)
inches	x	2.54	=	centimetres (cm)
inches	x	25.40	=	millimetres (mm)
inches	x	.0254	=	metres (m)
centimetres	x	.3937	=	inches
metres	x	1.0936	=	yards

INCHES INTO MILLIMETRES & CENTIMETRES (Rounded off slightly)

inches	mm	cm	inches	cm	inches	cm	inches	cm
1/8	3	0.3	5	12.5	21	53.5	38	96.5
1/4	6	0.6	5 1/2	14	22	56	39	99
3/8	10	1	6	15	23	58.5	40	101.5
1/2	13	1.3	7	18	24	61	41	104
5/8	15	1.5	8	20.5	25	63.5	42	106.5
3/4	20	2	9	23	26	66	43	109
7/8	22	2.2	10	25.5	27	68.5	44	112
1	25	2.5	11	28	28	71	45	114.5
1 1/4	32	3.2	12	30.5	29	73.5	46	117
1 1/2	38	3.8	13	33	30	76	47	119.5
1 3/4	45	4.5	14	35.5	31	79	48	122
2	50	5	15	38	32	81.5	49	124.5
2 1/2	65	6.5	16	40.5	33	84	50	127
3	75	7.5	17	43	34	86.5		
3 1/2	90	9	18	46	35	89		
4	100	10	19	48.5	36	91.5		
4 1/2	115	11.5	20	51	37	94		

Enchanted Forest

These wonderful handcrafted raku fired ceramic links and freshwater pearls are matched with a visually strong, large link chain. The stunning result this creates shows how easy it can be to make a fantastic piece using basic jewelry techniques.

1) Using wire flush cutters, cut chain to following lengths: 15 links, 11 links, four links and three links. ***Note:*** *If chain has closed links, find seam in chain link and cut at this point with wire flush cutters.*

2) The two shorter lengths will need a cut link on each end; the two longer lengths will need a cut link on one end.

3) Open end link on longest piece of chain; attach it to 50mm ceramic focal bead, close link.

4) In the same manner, connect remaining pieces ending with the following pattern: 15-link chain, 50mm ceramic focal bead, four-link chain, 30mm ceramic oval bead, three-link chain, 30mm ceramic oval and 11-link chain.

5) Slide one medium pearl or two small pearls onto head pin; make a wrapped loop. Trim excess wire. Repeat with all head pins and pearls.

6) Open a small jump ring, slide on the following: donut spacer, beaded head pin, donut spacer, beaded head pin, donut spacer and beaded head pin. Close jump ring. Repeat with all nine small jump rings.

MATERIALS
Ceramic 2-hole beads:
    50mm focal,
    2 (30mm) oval
30–40 assorted freshwater
    pearls, to match
    ceramic pieces
9 (11mm) antiqued silver
    metal disc charms
36 (6mm) silver donut
    spacers
27 (1½-inch) 24-gauge
    silver head pins

Antique silver oval jump
    rings: 18 small (7 x 5mm),
    2 large (10 x 8mm)
Antique silver toggle clasp
18 inches antique silver
    decorative 15mm round
    link chain
Round-nose pliers
2 pairs of chain-nose pliers
Wire flush cutters

FINISHED SIZE
22½ inches (including clasp)

7) Open beaded jump ring, attach it to 11-link chain four links from oval ceramic bead. In the same manner, attach another beaded jump ring to 11-link chain two links from oval ceramic bead.

8) In the same manner, attach the remaining seven beaded jump rings to the following: center link on three-link chain, both center links of four-link chain, second link from ceramic focal bead and every other link after that on 15-link chain.

9) Slide one round disc charm onto a small oval jump ring. Repeat until there are nine charms on jump rings.

10) Place each of these charms on same links as beaded jump rings (Photo A).

11) Attach toggle clasp to ends of chain using two large jump rings. ●

Photo A

Sources: *Ceramic beads from Jeff Barber; freshwater pearls from Artbeads.com; forged metal discs from Plaid Enterprises Inc.; Treasure Chest Chain, Lost and Found toggle clasp, Lost and Found assorted oval jump rings and 6mm donut spacers from Blue Moon Beads.*

Forged Fashion

The process of shaping metal by hammering is called forging. With a wonderful clasp as a focal and a variety of forged shapes and large rings, no one will know that making this necklace is as simple as opening and closing jump rings.

Project Note: *The toggle will be worn in front as the focal piece for this necklace.*

1) Using two pairs of chain-nose pliers, open a 12mm silver jump ring; slide on two copper jump rings; close jump ring. Repeat with remaining 12mm jump rings.

2) Linked jump rings will be attached between every large hammered link. Open and close copper jump rings on linked jump rings to connect hammered links as follows: copper rectangle, two silver ovals, copper rectangle, three silver ovals, copper rectangle, three silver ovals, copper rectangle, two silver ovals and a copper rectangle (Photo A).

Photo A

3) Create charms by opening a 4mm copper jump ring, sliding on a small hammered link and closing jump ring. Repeat this process,

attaching a 4mm copper jump ring to each of the following small hammered links: four gold squares, four silver squares, four copper rectangles, two silver ovals and two copper ovals.

4) Attach charms in pairs to first four 12mm jump rings starting at one end of linked chain as follows: gold square and silver oval, copper rectangle and silver square, copper oval and gold square and a silver square and copper rectangle. Repeat on other end (Photo B).

Photo B

5) Connect the following: 4mm copper jump ring, 6mm silver jump ring, 4mm copper jump ring, 6mm silver jump ring, 4mm copper jump and bar side of clasp.

6) Connect the following: remaining linked jump rings, 6mm silver jump ring, 4mm copper jump ring and remaining end of clasp.

7) Connect first copper jump ring on each linked clasp to a copper square on each end of linked chain. ●

Sources: *Hammered shapes from Funky Hannah's; hammered toggle clasp by Darice Inc.; Metal Madness large silver jump rings from Hirschberg Schutz & Co.; small silver jump rings from Fire Mountain Gems and Beads; copper jump rings from Rona Horn Designs.*

MATERIALS
Hammered links:
  5 (18 x 20mm) copper rectangles, 4 (18 x 6mm) copper rectangles, 2 (12 x 8mm) copper ovals, 10 (16 x 24mm) silver ovals, 2 (12 x 8mm) silver ovals, 4 (9mm) sliver squares, 4 (9mm) gold squares

Jump rings: 3 (6mm) silver, 15 (12mm) silver, 50 (4mm) copper
Large hammered silver toggle
2 pairs of chain-nose pliers

FINISHED SIZE
27 inches (including clasp)

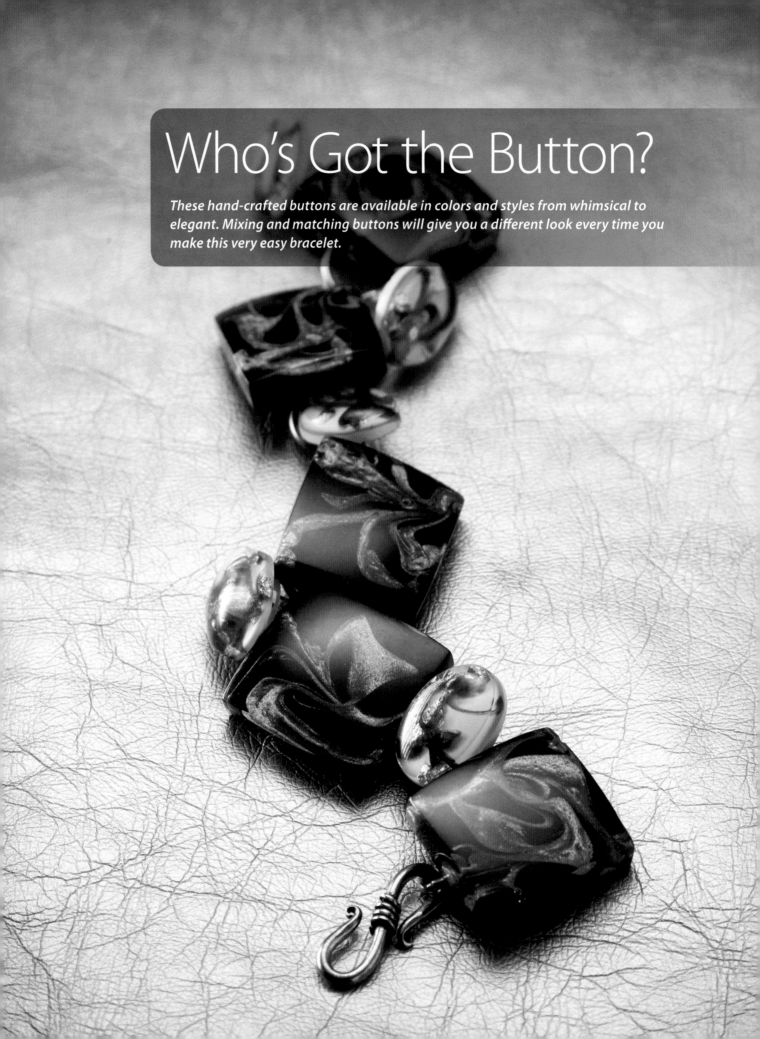

Who's Got the Button?

These hand-crafted buttons are available in colors and styles from whimsical to elegant. Mixing and matching buttons will give you a different look every time you make this very easy bracelet.

1) Using two pairs of chain-nose pliers, open 4mm jump ring, attach to loop on the back of an oval button, close jump ring. Repeat for all buttons.

2) In the same manner, open 9mm jump ring; slide on 4mm jump ring on a square button and 4mm jump ring on an oval button. Close jump ring.

3) Repeat step 2 to connect all buttons, alternating between squares and ovals. Finish with 9mm jump ring on each end (Photo A).

4) Attach the "S" clasp to the 9mm jump ring on each end. ●

Sources: *Buttons from Gail Hughes; "S" clasp from Fire Mountain Gems and Beads; copper jump rings from Rona Horn Designs.*

MATERIALS

Buttons: 5 large square,
   5 small oval
Copper jump rings:
   10 (4mm) 18-gauge,
   10 (9mm) 16-gauge

Copper "S" clasp
2 pairs of chain-nose pliers

FINISHED SIZE

7¼ inches (including
   clasp)

Photo A

Around the Bend

The geometric shapes of the rectangles along with the triangular jump rings are a fun contrast to the hammered circles and wavy disks. They all come together to make a great necklace that is suitable for business or casual wear.

1) Using two pairs of chain-nose pliers, open jump ring, slide on two jump rings; close jump ring. Repeat until there are six sets of three jump rings.

2) Sets of three jump rings are used to connect metal rectangles and circles. Do this by opening end jump ring in a set of three, attaching a shape and close jump ring. Attach shapes as follows: small gunmetal rectangle, three jump rings, medium brass rectangle, three jump rings, large gunmetal rectangle and three jump rings.

3) For other side, attach shapes as follows: small brass rectangle, three jump rings, medium gunmetal rectangle, three jump rings, large brass rectangle and three jump rings.

4) Stack three hammered circles on top of each other. Open last jump ring from step 2, attach to stacked circles, close jump ring. Repeat with last jump ring from step 3.

5) Attach a jump ring to rectangles at each end.

6) Cut chain into two 12-inch lengths.

7) Open a jump ring; slide on end link of a length of chain. Loop chain through an end triangle jump ring from step 5. Slide end link on remaining end of chain onto open jump ring; close jump ring. Repeat on other side.

8) Attach lobster-claw clasp to a jump ring from step 7; remaining step 7 jump ring acts as other side of clasp.

9) Using a jump ring, attach a wavy disk to bottom of three stacked circles. Repeat until all eight disks are attached to circles. ●

Sources: *Rectangles and hammered circles from Beadbury; rolo chain from Funky Hannah's; Forged wavy disks from Plaid Enterprises Inc.; jump rings from Michaels Stores Inc.*

MATERIALS
Gunmetal rectangles:
    1 small (20 x 13mm),
    1 medium (22 x 18mm),
    1 large (36 x 20mm)
Brass rectangles: 1 small
    (20 x 13mm), 1 medium
    (22 x 18mm), 1 large
    (36 x 20mm)
3 (30mm) silver hammered
    circles
8 (11mm) mixed metal
    wavy disks

30 (6mm) silver triangle
    jump rings
18mm silver lobster-claw
    clasp
24 inches brass rolo chain
2 pairs of chain-nose pliers
Wire flush cutters

FINISHED SIZE
25¼ inches (including
    clasp)

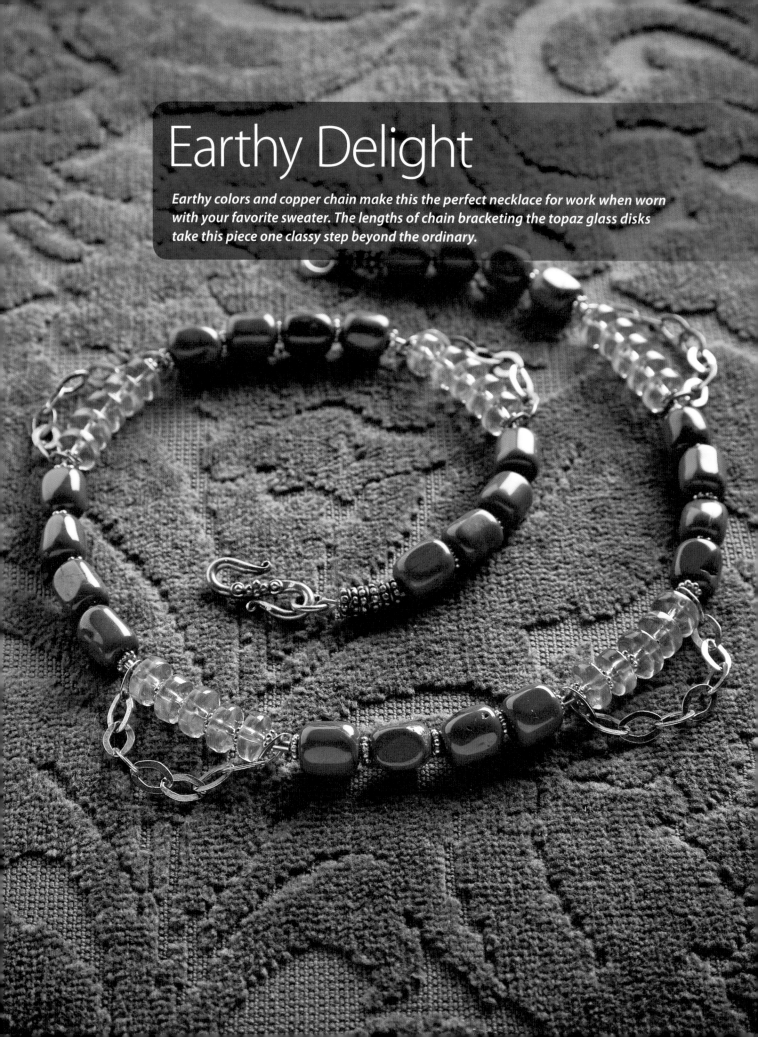

Earthy Delight

Earthy colors and copper chain make this the perfect necklace for work when worn with your favorite sweater. The lengths of chain bracketing the topaz glass disks take this piece one classy step beyond the ordinary.

1) Cut copper chain into five 2-inch pieces.

2) String crimp bead onto beading wire ½ inch from end; string beading wire through loop on end of clasp and back through crimp bead. Flatten crimp bead with crimping pliers. Trim excess wire.

3) String three double rondelles.

4) String a red jasper nugget and a spacer. Repeat three times.

5) String a tube bead. Slide end link of a 2-inch piece of chain over tube bead.

6) String a spacer and a topaz disk. Repeat four times.

7) String a spacer and a tube bead. Slide other end of chain over tube bead (Photo A).

Photo A

8) String a spacer.

9) Repeat steps 4–8 four times.

10) String a red jasper nugget and a spacer. Repeat two times.

11) String a jasper nugget, three double rondelles and a crimp bead.

12) String beading wire through loop on other end of clasp and back through crimp bead. Flatten crimp bead with crimping pliers. Trim excess wire. ●

Sources: *Red jasper nuggets, copper rondelle spacers and copper tubes from Fire Mountain Gems and Beads; Beading Times topaz glass disks from Michaels Stores Inc.; copper chain and clasp from Rings & Things; beading wire from Soft Flex Co.*

MATERIALS
24 (7–9mm) red jasper nuggets
25 (8 x 5mm) topaz glass disks
58 (5mm) copper spacers
6 (6mm) copper double rondelles
10 (2 x 3mm) copper tube beads
2 copper crimp beads
Copper S clasp
11 inches (8mm) flat copper chain
24 inches .024-inch-diameter nylon-coated flexible beading wire
Crimping pliers
Wire flush cutters

FINISHED SIZE
19½ inches (including clasp)

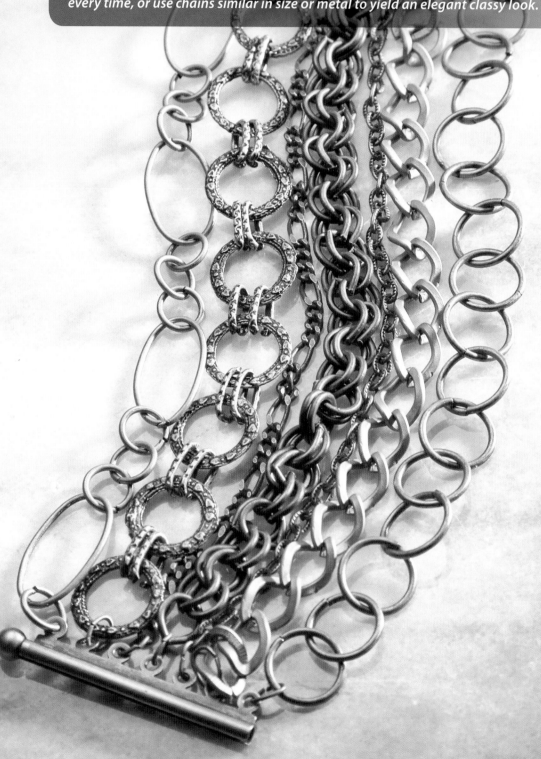

Elemental Metal

This is the perfect project for a beginner, and a very fast and fun project for those with more experience. Use a wide variety of chains for a piece that will get compliments every time, or use chains similar in size or metal to yield an elegant classy look.

Project note: *The shortest length will deter- mine length of bracelet. The clasp and rings will add approximately 1 inch. The bracelet will have a tighter fit due to width of chains and slack needed to open and close clasp, so cut chains a bit longer than needed. Lengths can always be shortened if needed. A three- or five-strand clasp can give you a daintier look. All of them are very comfortable to wear.*

1) Using memory wire shears, cut each chain into 6½–7-inch lengths or longer if desired.

2) Lay chains out in desired order for finished bracelet, alternating size and color.

3) Use jump ring to attach first chain to first loop on clasp. Attach other end to correspond- ing loop on other side of clasp in the same manner. Repeat for each remaining chain. ●

Sources: *Chains from Michaels Stores Inc.; brass slide clasp from Ornamentea.*

MATERIALS
7 (9-inch) lengths of
    assorted styles of chain
    in brass, copper and
    antique silver
14 (7 x 5mm) antique
    silver oval jump rings
7-strand antique brass
    slide clasp

2 pairs of chain-nose pliers
Memory wire shears

FINISHED SIZE
7–9 inches (including
    clasp)

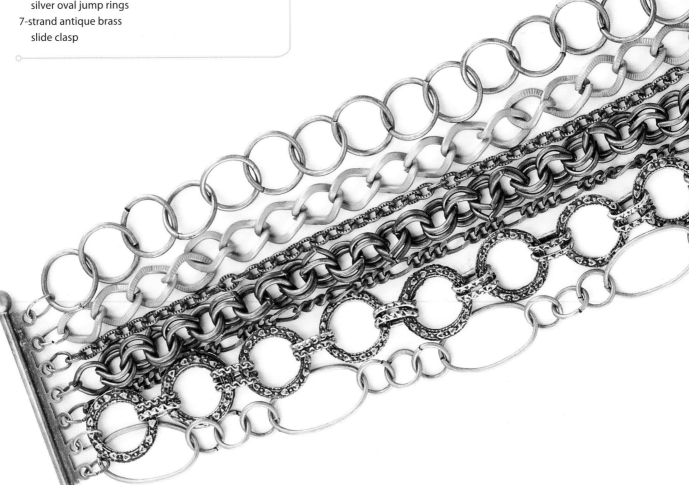

Be Mused Be Inspired

Large link chain, metal tokens and tiger's-eye rounds make a great visual statement. Only seven from the set of 12 tokens are used, allowing you to make your own personal statement when you wear it with this very simple necklace.

1) Open one 8 x 6mm jump ring and slide it through last links on one end of both chains to connect them together. Repeat on other end of chains. Attach ball-and-socket clasp to each end of connected chains with two more 8 x 6mm jump rings (Photo A).

Photo A

2) Choose seven Muse tokens to use in necklace. Find center of brass chain; attach one Muse token to center link using a 10 x 8mm jump ring. Continue adding tokens every third link to left and right of center token until all are attached.

3) Slide one tiger's-eye bead onto a head pin; use round-nose pliers to form a wrapped loop above bead. Repeat for remaining beads.

4) Find center of steel chain. Attach first two beaded head pins ¼ inch to left and right of center of chain using an 8 x 6mm jump ring. Attach remaining beaded head pins in every third link to left and right of first two beads. ●

Sources: *Muse tokens from Tim Holtz; Natural Elegance brass and steel chain and Lost & Found assorted oval jump rings from Blue Moon Beads; tiger's-eye beads from Fire Mountain Gems and Beads.*

MATERIALS
1 package Muse tokens
10 (10mm) tiger's-eye round beads
Antique silver oval jump rings: 14 (8 x 6mm), 7 (10 x 8mm)
10 silver head pins
Gunmetal ball-and-socket clasp

18 inches (9 x 14mm) steel chain
20 inches (8 x 16mm) oval brass chain
Round-nose pliers
2 pairs of chain-nose pliers
Wire flush cutters

FINISHED SIZE
19½ inches (including clasp)

Black Tie Glamour

The combination of all the shapes and sizes of beads, along with sections that have two strands, make this necklace really stand out in a crowd. The clear beads catch and reflect the light while the rich black pillows and drops enhance all the sparkle.

Necklace

1) Cut two 35-inch pieces of beading wire. Holding two strands together, string a crimp bead ½ inch from end. String both ends through a closed jump ring and back through crimp bead. Flatten crimp bead with crimping pliers. Connect lobster-claw clasp to closed jump ring by using two pairs of chain-nose pliers to open jump ring on clasp. Attach opened loop to closed jump ring and close.

2) Hold two strands together. String beads as follows: black pillow bead, three bicone beads, black pillow bead and three round cut crystal beads.

3) Separate two strands. String five black drop beads onto each strand.

4) Hold two strands together. String beads as follows: three bicone beads and a black pillow bead.

5) Separate two strands. Slide five long glass nuggets onto each strand.

NECKLACE MATERIALS

48 (9mm) matte black glass drops
10 (12mm) black pillow glass beads
16 (10mm) clear round cut crystal glass beads
18 (8 x 15mm) clear bicone glass beads
46 (8 x 20mm) clear side-drilled long glass nuggets
2 (4mm) closed silver jump rings
13mm 14-gauge silver jump ring
2 (1.8mm) crimp beads
18mm sterling silver lobster-claw clasp
70 inches .024-inch-diameter beading wire
Round-nose pliers
2 pairs of chain-nose pliers
Crimping pliers
Wire flush cutters

FINISHED SIZE
31 inches (including clasp)

6) Hold two strands together. String beads as follows: black pillow bead and five round cut crystal beads.

7) Separate the strands. String seven black drops onto each strand.

8) Hold strands together. String beads as follows: three bicone beads and a black pillow bead.

9) Separate the strands. String 13 long glass nuggets onto each strand.

10) Repeat steps 2–8 in reverse.

11) String both strands through a crimp bead, a closed jump ring and back through crimp bead; flatten crimp bead using crimping pliers.

12) Using two pairs of chain-nose pliers, open 13mm jump ring. Slide through closed jump ring and close.

Earrings

1) Cut a 2-inch piece of silver wire. Using round-nose pliers, form a simple loop on one end. Slide on a clear bicone bead. Form a simple loop next to bead.

2) Cut a 2-inch piece of silver wire. Slide on black drop bead, 1-inch from end. Using round-nose pliers, form a **briolette wrap** with a wrapped loop. Cross one tail of wire across the other, forming the starting point for a wrap, while forcing other wire to center vertically above bead, Step A *(see illustration).* Wrap crossed wire tail around vertical wire; trim excess wire, Step B *(see illustration).* Form a simple loop with vertical wire using round-nose pliers; trim excess wire, Step C *(see illustration).*

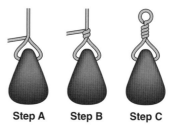

Step A   Step B   Step C

Briolette Wrap

3) Open a simple loop on clear bicone wire; attach briolette wrap; close loop.

4) To attach bicone bead wire to ear wire; open top loop, string through loop on ear wire and close loop.

5) Repeat steps 1–4 for second earring. ●

Sources: *Drop beads from Beaded Impressions Inc.; pillow beads from Beadaholique; round cut and bicone beads from The Bead Gallery; silver jump rings from Fire Mountain Gems and Beads; beading wire from Soft Flex Co.*

EARRINGS MATERIALS
2 (9mm) matte black glass drops
2 (8 x 15mm) clear bicone glass beads
8 inches 20-gauge sterling silver wire

2 sterling silver fishhook ear wires
Round-nose pliers
Wire flush cutters

FINISHED SIZE
2 inches long

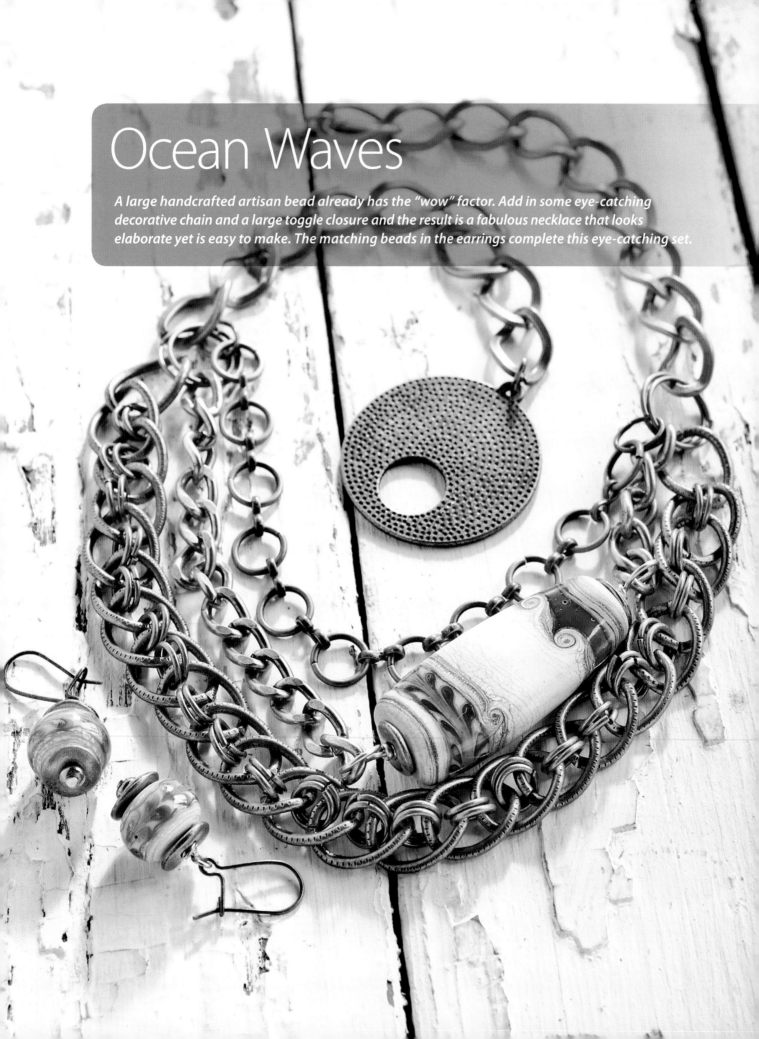

Ocean Waves

A large handcrafted artisan bead already has the "wow" factor. Add in some eye-catching decorative chain and a large toggle closure and the result is a fabulous necklace that looks elaborate yet is easy to make. The matching beads in the earrings complete this eye-catching set.

Project note: Thick chains can damage wire flush cutters, use memory wire shears when needed for cutting thicker chains.

Necklace

1) Using memory wire shears, cut chains to the following lengths: large flat curb chain two 7-inch lengths and large curb chain one 4-inch length and one 1¾-inch length.

2) Using round-nose pliers, start to form a wrapped loop on one end of brass wire, stopping before wrapping tail. Insert formed loop into end link of 1¾-inch length of chain, finish wrapping loop (Photo A).

Photo A

3) Slide onto brass wire a wavy donut bead, 45mm lampwork bead and a wavy donut bead.

4) Start to form wrapped loop on this end of brass wire, stopping before wrapping tail. Insert formed loop into last link of the 4-inch length of wire, finish wrapping loop.

5) Using two pairs of chain-nose pliers, open 10 x 8mm jump ring, slip on last link of circle link chain, close. Repeat for other end of circle link chain.

NECKLACE MATERIALS
45mm handcrafted
   lampwork bead
2 (11mm) brass wavy donuts
4 (13mm) round brass
   jump rings
2 (10 x 8mm) large brass
   oval jump rings
2 (8 x 6mm) medium brass
   oval jump rings
Large decorative brass
   toggle clasp
6 inches 18-gauge
   brass wire

Antique gold chain:
   16 inches large flat curb,
   6 inches circle link chain
Brass chain: 6 inches large
   curb, 9 inches large
   decorative chain
Round-nose pliers
2 pairs of chain-nose pliers
Memory wire shears

FINISHED SIZE
19 inches (including clasp)

6) Open one 13mm round jump ring. Slide on the following: jump ring on last link of circle link chain, last link of chain with lampwork bead attached, last link of decorative chain and last link on 7-inch piece of flat curb chain. Close the jump ring. Repeat with second jump ring for additional strength.

7) Repeat step 6 on the other ends of chain; not attaching other end of 7-inch flat curb chain used in step 6. Instead attach last link on remaining 7-inch piece of large flat curb chain.

8) Attach toggle clasp to ends of 7-inch pieces of flat curb chain using two 8 x 6mm oval jump rings.

Earrings

1) On head pin slide a gold rondelle, wavy donut bead, 10 x 14mm lampwork bead and a wavy donut bead. Using round-nose pliers, form a wrapped loop. If hole in wavy disk is too large to be held in place with finish wrap, continue wrapping wire in a circle to form a

spiral on top of wavy donut to hold it in place. Slide finished dangle onto ear wire (Photo B).

Photo B

2) Repeat for the second earring. ●

Sources: *Focal bead and earring beads by Julie Nordine; Forged brass toggle and wavy donuts from Plaid Enterprises Inc.; Lost and Found jump rings and earwires from Blue Moon Beads; Bead Landing chains from Michaels Stores, Inc.*

EARRINGS MATERIALS
2 (10 x 14mm) hand
    crafted lampwork beads
4 (11mm) brass wavy
    donuts
2 (4.5mm) gold rondelle
    beads
2 gold head pins

2 antique gold kidney ear
    wires
Round-nose pliers
Wire flush cutters

FINISHED SIZE
1⅜ inches long

Romantic Memory

This fun necklace uses simple materials and simple construction. The resin beads come in this wonderful mix which makes putting the necklace together fast and easy without having to wade through all the color and shape decisions before you begin.

Project note: *If making both necklace and earrings, set aside four beads for the earrings before you begin the necklace.*

Necklace

1) Slide a resin bead onto a head pin. Using round-nose pliers, form a simple loop large enough to fit over 2.5mm rubber tubing. Repeat for all resin beads. If bead holes are too big for head pins, slide on an 11-0 seed bead first then resin bead.

2) Set aside four small beaded head pins to be used for the back of necklace.

3) Using round-nose pliers, form a simple loop on one end of memory wire. Slide the 17-inch piece of rubber tubing over the memory wire to make necklace base.

4) Slide beaded head pins over necklace base. If mix contains donut beads, slide onto necklace through center hole. If mix contains a pendant bead, connect it to necklace base with optional large jump ring (Photo A).

Photo A

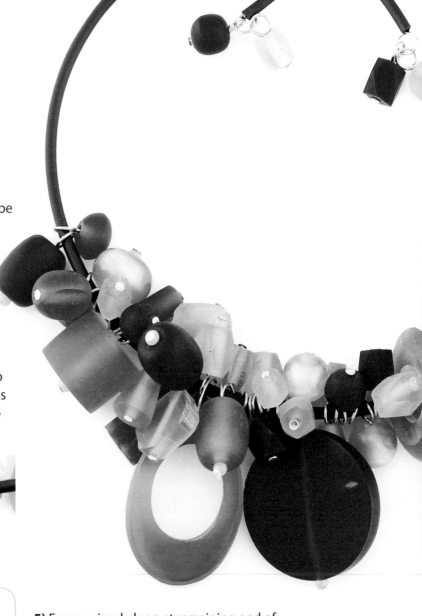

NECKLACE MATERIALS
40-55 mixed purple resin beads
25 (11-0) seed beads to match
13mm silver jump ring (optional)
50 (2-inch) silver head pins
17 inches (2.5mm) rubber tubing
20 inches necklace memory wire
Round-nose pliers
2 pairs of chain-nose pliers
Wire flush cutters
Memory wire shears

FINISHED SIZE
16 inches

5) Form a simple loop at remaining end of memory wire; trim excess memory wire or rubber tubing.

6) Using two pairs of chain-nose pliers, open loops on beaded head pins from step 2 and attach two to each loop at back of necklace.

Earrings

1) Slide one resin bead on a head pin; form a simple loop.

2) Slide one seed bead, resin bead and a seed bead onto a head pin, form a simple loop.

3) Cut head off one head pin, form a simple loop. Slide on a seed bead, a ½-inch piece of rubber tubing and a seed bead. Form a simple loop.

4) Repeat step 3 with a ³⁄₁₆-inch piece of rubber tubing.

5) Attach beaded head pin from step 1 to head pin from step 3.

6) Attach beaded head pin from step 2 to head pin from step 4.

7) Attach both pieces from step 5 and 6 to the ear wire.

8) Repeat for the second earring. ●

Sources: *Rubber tubing and necklace memory wire from Beadalon; resin bead mix from Natural Touch Beads.*

EARRINGS MATERIALS
4 mixed purple
   resin beads
12 (11-0) seed beads
   to match
8 (2-inch) silver head pins
2.5mm rubber tubing:
   2 (½-inch) pieces,
   2 (³⁄₁₆-inch) pieces

2 silver round ear wires
Round-nose pliers
Wire flush cutters

FINISHED SIZE
2¼ inches long

Black & White & Bold

This fun black-and-white set makes a bold statement and all the movement of the handcrafted lampwork beads makes it fun to wear.

Bracelet

1) Using split ring, attach clasp to end of chain.

2) Slide a rondelle spacer, 16 x 11mm lampwork bead and a rondelle spacer onto a head pin. Using round-nose pliers begin to form a wrapped loop but do not wrap loop yet. Wrap will be completed in step 4. Repeat eight times.

3) Slide a coin bead onto a head pin. Begin to form a wrapped loop but do not wrap loop yet. Repeat with all remaining coin beads.

4) Slide a lampwork dangle from step 2 onto chain five links from clasp. Complete wrapped loop, connecting lampwork dangle to chain. Repeat with remaining lampwork dangles every sixth link.

5) In the same manner, attach a 6mm white coin dangle, 12mm black coin dangle and a 6mm white coin dangle to chain, spaced evenly between first two lampwork dangles (Photo A).

BRACELET MATERIALS
9 (16 x 11mm) handcrafted lampwork beads
Coin beads: 8 (6mm) white, 10 (6mm) black, 5 (8mm) white, 4 (12mm) black
18 (3mm) silver rondelle spacers
7½ inches silver chain
36 (3mm) silver jump rings (optional)

6mm silver split ring
36 silver head pins
Silver lobster-claw clasp
Round-nose pliers
2 pairs of chain-nose pliers
Wire flush cutters

FINISHED SIZE
7–8½ inches (including clasp)

Photo A

6) In the same manner, attach a 6mm black coin dangle, 8mm white coin dangle and a 6mm black coin dangle to chain, spaced evenly between next two lampwork dangles.

7) Repeat steps 5–6 along length of chain, finishing between last two lampwork dangles.

8) Attach two 6mm black coin dangles and an 8mm white coin dangle to last link on end of chain. Extra chain between last lampwork dangle and end of chain makes bracelet adjustable.

Project note: Instead of wrapping beaded dangles directly onto chain, complete wrapped loops on beaded dangles and attach them to chain using optional jump rings. Using jump rings will make completing the bracelet quicker; however, attaching beaded dangles to chain with wrapped loops will create a more secure link.

Earrings

1) Slide a rondelle spacer, 10 x 8mm lampwork bead and a rondelle spacer onto a head pin. Form wrapped loop. Slide lampwork dangle onto an earring hoop.

2) Repeat step 1 for second earring. ●

Sources: *Handcrafted lampwork beads from Rona Horn Designs; coin beads from The Bead Monkey; rondelles and jump rings from Fire Mountain Gems and Beads; clasp and chain from Thunderbird Supply Co.*

EARRINGS MATERIALS

2 (10 x 8mm) handcrafted lampwork beads
4 (3mm) silver rondelle spacers
2 silver head pins

2 (20mm) earring hoops
Round-nose pliers
Wire flush cutters

FINISHED SIZE
1 inch long

Drops of Honey

The small silver tubes, drop beads and tiny silver beads give this a very elegant and feminine look. Making it a three-strand necklace with the twisted tubes and handcrafted lampwork beads creates a more complex look than it is.

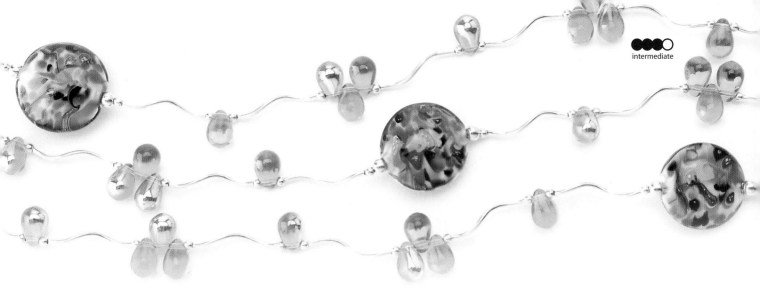

Project note: *The 2mm silver beads keep the silver tubes from sliding into the amber drops and lampwork beads.*

Necklace

1) Using two pairs of chain-nose pliers, open jump ring; slide on eye side of clasp; close jump ring.

2) String crimp bead onto one 20-inch length of beading wire ½ inch from end; string beading wire through jump ring and back through crimp bead. Flatten crimp bead with chain-nose pliers.

3) String four 3mm beads and a 2mm bead.

NECKLACE MATERIALS
3 (20mm) lampwork glass lentil beads
76 (9mm) amber AB drops
Round silver beads: 92 (2mm), 30 (3mm)
46 (1 x 17mm) sterling silver plain spiral tubes
6 (1.3mm) silver crimp beads
5mm silver jump ring
25mm silver hook-and-eye clasp

3 (20-inch) lengths .014-inch-diameter nylon-coated flexible beading wire
Round-nose pliers
2 pairs of chain-nose pliers
Wire flush cutters

FINISHED SIZE
19 inches (including clasp)

4) String beads as follows: spiral tube, 2mm bead, three drop beads, 2mm bead, spiral tube, 2mm bead, drop bead, 2mm bead, spiral tube, 2mm bead, three drop beads, 2mm bead, spiral tube, 2mm bead, drop bead and a 2mm.

5) String a spiral tube, 2mm bead, 3mm bead, lampwork bead, 3mm bead, 2mm bead and a spiral tube.

6) Repeat step 4 in reverse until there are nine more tubes strung.

7) String a 2mm bead, four 3mm beads and a crimp bead. Insert wire through hook end of clasp and back through crimp bead. Flatten crimp bead with chain-nose pliers. Trim excess wire.

8) Beginning on hook clasp end, repeat steps 2–7 crimping wire onto jump ring. ***Note:*** *Before attaching end to jump ring, wrap second strand loosely around first strand.*

9) For third strand, repeat step 2.

10) String beads as follows: four 3mm beads, 2mm bead, spiral tube, 2mm bead, drop bead, 2mm bead, spiral tube, 2mm bead, three drop beads, 2mm bead, spiral tube and a 2mm bead.

11) String a drop bead, 2mm bead, spiral tube, 2mm bead, three drop beads, 2mm bead, spiral tube, 2mm bead, drop bead, 2mm bead, spiral tube, 2mm bead, three drop beads, 2mm bead, spiral tube, 2mm bead, drop bead, 2mm bead and a spiral tube.

12) String a 2mm bead, 3mm bead, lampwork bead, 3mm bead and a 2mm bead.

13) Repeat steps 10 and 11 in reverse.

14) Wrap strand loosely around first and second strands once. Insert wire through hook end of clasp and back through crimp bead. Flatten crimp bead with chain-nose pliers. Trim excess wire (Photo A).

Photo A

Earrings

1) String a crimp bead onto one 3-inch piece of beading wire ½ inch from end. Insert wire through loop on ear wire and back through crimp bead. Flatten crimp with chain-nose pliers.

2) String beads as follows: 3mm bead, 2mm bead, spiral tube, 2mm bead, 3mm bead, crimp bead and a drop bead.

3) Insert wire back through crimp bead and 3mm bead, forming a loop that drop bead will dangle from.

4) Flatten crimp bead with chain-nose pliers. Trim excess wire.

5) Repeat steps 1–4 for second earring. ●

EARRINGS MATERIALS
2 (9mm) amber AB drops
Round silver beads: 4 (2mm), 4 (3mm)
2 (1 x 17mm) sterling silver plain spiral tubes
4 (1.3mm) silver crimp beads
2 silver round ear wires

2 (3-inch) lengths .014-inch-diameter nylon-coated flexible beading wire
Chain-nose pliers

FINISHED SIZE
2½ inches long

Sources: *Handcrafted lampwork glass lentil beads from Rona Horn Designs; drop beads from Beaded Impressions Inc.; silver beads from Rings & Things; spiral tubes from Monsterslayer Inc.; clasp hook, ear wires and jump rings from Fire Mountain Gems and Beads; beading wire from Soft Flex Co.*

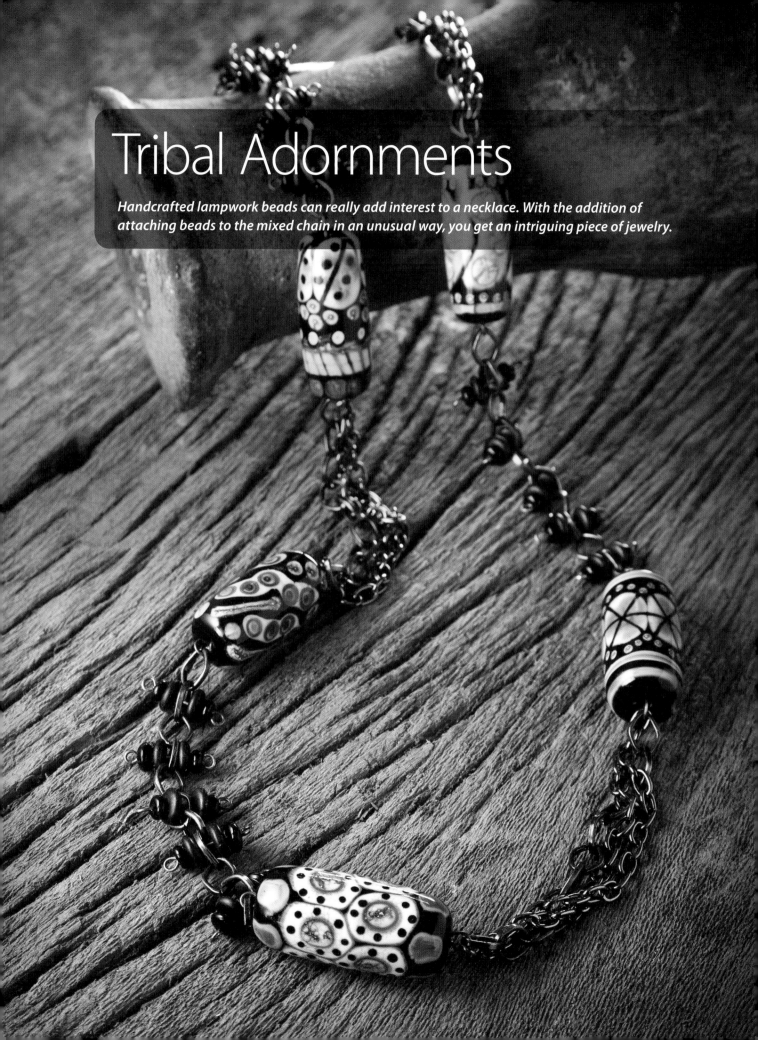

Tribal Adornments

Handcrafted lampwork beads can really add interest to a necklace. With the addition of attaching beads to the mixed chain in an unusual way, you get an intriguing piece of jewelry.

Project Note: *Because this necklace has no clasp, the final length should be approximately 24 inches or long enough to fit over your head. The final length may vary depending on the lampwork beads and the chain used.*

1) Cut the head off a head pin; using round-nose pliers, form a simple loop. Slide on a lampwork bead, form another simple loop at this end of bead. Repeat remaining five lampwork beads.

2) Cut large oval chain into six 2¾-inch lengths. **Note:** *This section of chain will need to have an odd number of links.*

3) Cut small oval chain into six 3-inch lengths.

4) Using two pairs of chain-nose pliers, open simple loop on a beaded head pin. Insert opened loop into an end link of large oval chain, close loop. Repeat this process until all beaded head pins are connected by lengths of large oval chain. Finish by attaching the last length of chain to the first beaded head pin making a complete circle.

MATERIALS
6 (30mm) cylinder
   lampwork beads
Gunmetal oval chain:
   18 inches (6 x 8mm)
   large links, 18 inches
   (3.5 x 5.5mm) small links
Black rondelle beads: 30
   (4mm) matte, 30 (6mm)

15 (2-inch) antique silver
   head pins
Round-nose pliers
2 pairs of chain-nose pliers
Wire flush cutters

FINISHED SIZE
25 inches

5) In the same manner, attach two lengths of small chain to a section between two beaded head pins. Repeat in every other section of chain.

6) This step will be worked in sections where there is only one length of large oval chain. Cut the head off a head pin. Form a small simple loop on one end. Slide on a 4mm rondelle and a 6mm rondelle. Insert wire through the second link of large oval chain from a beaded head pin. Slide on a 6mm rondelle and a 4mm rondelle. Form a small simple loop, leaving approximately ⅛ inch between the 6mm rondelles. Repeat in every other link in this section of chain

7) Repeat step 6 in the other two sections where there is only one length of large oval chain. ●

Sources: *Handcrafted lampwork beads from AMR GlassWorks; Natural Elegance head pins and chains from Blue Moon Beads; rondelle glass beads from The Beadin' Path.*

Wonderful Brass Windows

Mixing different components and simple techniques can result in a design that seems so much more than the pieces you put into it. The multiple strands and the large pendant make this a great statement piece that isn't as difficult as it appears.

Project note: *In this project crimp beads are flattened very close to end of wire. Since they are covered by the cone, it is simpler to flatten them rather than using the usual crimping method.*

1) String crimp bead onto one 24-inch length of beading wire ½ inch from end; string back through crimp bead creating a small loop. Flatten crimp bead with chain-nose pliers (*see illustration*).

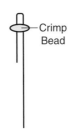

—Crimp Bead

Crimping

MATERIALS
Amber and stone brass
    pendant
Glass window beads: 20
    (12 x 14mm) faceted
    amber, 22 (10 x 15mm)
    table cut crystal, 10
    (22mm) top drilled
    amber marquis
225 (11/0) Czech hex-cut
    copper iris seed beads
6 brass crimps
2 (12mm) brass cones
Small brass toggle

4 inches 20-gauge brass or
    gold tone wire
5 inches brass cable chain
.024-inch-diameter nylon-
    coated flexible beading
    wire: 3 (24-inch) lengths
Round-nose pliers
2 pairs of chain-nose pliers
Wire flush cutters

FINISHED SIZE
20½ inches (including
    clasp)

2) String on faceted amber bead and seed bead. Repeat until all faceted amber beads are strung, ending with faceted amber bead. String on crimp bead, string line back through crimp bead; in the same manner as step 1, flatten crimp bead.

3) Repeat step 1 on a second strand of beading wire.

4) String on table cut crystal bead and seed bead. Repeat until all table cut crystal beads are strung, ending with table cut crystal bead. String on crimp bead, string line back through crimp bead; in the same manner as step 1 flatten crimp bead.

5) Repeat step 1 on a third strand of beading wire.

6) String 28 seed beads.

7) String amber marquis bead and 13 seed beads onto beading wire. Repeat three times.

8) String amber marquis bead and 40 seed beads onto the beading wire. Slide the pendant over the seed beads.

9) Repeat step 7.

10) String an amber marquis bead and 28 seed beads. String on crimp bead, string line back through crimp bead; in the same manner as step 1 flatten crimp bead.

11) Cut the 5 inches of 20-gauge wire into two equal pieces.

12) Using round-nose pliers start to form a wrapped loop on one end of wire, stopping before wrapping tail. Insert loops on one end of each strand of beading wire into the formed loop, finish wrapping loop (Photo A).

13) Slide the brass cone onto the wire until it covers crimp beads and sits firmly against the beads on each strand. Form a wrapped loop snug against the brass cone.

14) Repeat steps 12 and 13 for the other end of strands.

15) Cut the brass chain into two equal pieces. Open the end link of one piece of chain and attach it to the wrapped loop next to brass cone. Repeat with the second piece on other side.

16) Attach brass toggle closure to each end of the chain in the same manner as step 15. ●

Sources: *Global Nomad pendant from Blue Moon Beads; window beads from Halcraft USA; hex seed beads from Turtle Island Beads; chain from Thunderbird Supply Co.; brass cones from Ornamentea; beading wire from Soft Flex Co.*

Photo A

Autumn Medley

Just a few knots and a combination of several basic jewelry techniques result in this unique necklace. This piece can be easily changed to represent spring, summer or winter just by choosing a different mix of fibers.

Project note: *Use faux suede, silk cord, pearl cotton, yarn and embroidery fibers in your choice of colors.*

1) Use round-nose pliers to form a wrapped loop on one end of one 5-inch wire.

2) String beads on wire as follows: 5mm round bead, 8mm round bead, 12mm disk, 20mm round focal bead, 12mm disk, 8mm round bead and 5mm round bead. Make a wrapped loop next to last bead.

3) If loops are not facing same direction, hold one loop firmly with one pair of chain-nose pliers; grasp other loop with second pair of chain-nose pliers, turn gently until loops face same direction. Curve beaded wire slightly with fingers.

4) Hold 11 strands of mixed fibers together. Slide all 11 fibers through one wrapped loop on wire; fold in half. Make an **overhand knot** (*see illustration*) with all fibers 2½ inches from center fold. Make a second overhand knot 1½ inches from first knot. Set aside (Photo A).

Overhand Knot

Photo A

5) Hold remaining 11 mixed fibers together and slide them through remaining wrapped loop on silver wire; fold in half. Make an overhand knot 3½ inches from center fold.

MATERIALS

20mm round silver focal bead
Sterling silver dipped ceramic beads: 2 (12mm) disks, 2 (8mm) rounds
2 (5mm) sterling silver braided round beads
10 feet dark brown #5 pearl cotton
25-inch lengths of mixed fibers in coordinating autumn colors: 2 black faux suede, 2 light brown silk cord, 2 green silk cord, 8 dark brown #3 pearl cotton, 8 medium brown #5 pearl cotton
5 inches 14-gauge sterling silver wire
2 (9mm) silver cord ends
2 (6mm) silver jump rings
Silver ball-and-socket clasp
Round-nose pliers
2 pairs of chain-nose pliers
Wire flush cutters
Epoxy glue

FINISHED SIZE

20 inches (including clasp)

Make second overhand knot on top of first, creating a larger knot (Photo B).

Photo B

6) Cut a 5-foot strand of dark brown #5 pearl cotton to bind and knot loose ends of fibers. *Note: Length of cord used for binding will vary depending on the type of fibers used in necklace.* Starting 8 inches from the center fold, tie the binding strand in an overhand knot around all fibers. Wrap the **binding** (*see illustration*) strand tightly around all of the fibers. Do not make binding any longer than depth of cord **Binding** end and wrap enough fiber to make a snug fit into cord end. When finished binding, tie an overhand knot around all fibers and trim excess binding strand. Trim ends of fibers flush with end of binding. Repeat for other side of necklace.

7) Place enough glue to coat binding fiber and to make contact with inside of cord end; insert bound fiber into cord end. Immediately clean up extra glue not inside cord end. Repeat for other side. Set aside until completely dry.

8) Once dry, use jump rings to attach ball-and-socket clasp to cord ends (Photo C). ●

Photo C

Sources: *Wire and ceramic beads from Connie Fox; silver beads and cord ends from Rings & Things; silver jump rings from Fire Mountain Gems and Beads.*

Woodland Walk

The colors in this necklace were inspired by a painting with the same title. The base necklace has a very simple construction featuring stone rectangles and faceted peridot glass beads. Adding tied silk really completes the feeling of a sunlit forest.

Project note: *Silk string comes in strands 40 inches long.*

1) String beads onto beading line in the following order: crimp bead, faceted peridot bead, five seed beads, stone pillow bead, five seed beads. Repeat this pattern, leaving out crimp bead, until one faceted peridot bead and one stone pillow bead are left.

2) String a crimp bead, then continue stringing remaining beads; completing the pattern from step 1, ending with five seed beads.

3) Slide end of the beading wire from step 1 through beads and crimp bead on the other side of beading wire, making a complete circle. String other end of beading wire through crimp bead on beading wire from step 1. Carefully pull both tails until there are no more gaps between beads, creating a **crimped loop** (*see illustration*).

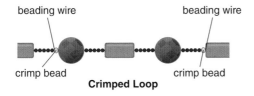

beading wire · beading wire

crimp bead · crimp bead

Crimped Loop

4) Using chain-nose pliers flatten each crimp bead.

5) Tuck the tails through next couple beads; trim off excess wire.

6) Cut the assorted colors of silk cord into 72 (4-inch) lengths. Tie a 4-inch length of silk cord into a **square knot** (*see illustration*) around a five seed bead section of necklace, pull tight. Repeat with two more lengths of silk cord in different colors. Repeat over each section of seed beads.

Square Knot

7) Trim silk cord ends to ½-inch to 1-inch long, varying lengths. ●

Sources: *Faceted glass beads from Halcraft USA; silk string from Silk Painting is Fun; beading wire from Soft Flex Co.*

MATERIALS

12 (18mm) round faceted peridot glass beads
12 (14 x 8mm) stone pillow beads
120 (8/0) seed beads
2 silver crimps
288 inches hand dyed silk string in 8 assorted fall colors

30 inches .024-inch-diameter nylon-coated flexible beading wire
Chain-nose pliers
Wire flush cutters

FINISHED SIZE

26 inches

Knot Right Now

This fun bracelet mixes basic macramé knots with lots of beads and a button closure. Since the bracelet base is made first, there is no need to decide on bead placement before you begin. The beads are all tied on after the base is completed.

Project note: *Having bracelet anchored while you work helps to make snug, even knots. To anchor your bracelet, you can use masking tape to attach piece firmly to a table top, T-pins to pin bracelet to cardboard, foam core or a piece of ceiling tile or a clip board.*

1. Cut two 36-inch lengths and one 132-inch length of dark brown waxed linen. Hold two 36-inch strands together; fold in half to find center. Fold 132-inch length in half. Make a **lark's head knot** over both long strands at center (*see illustration*).

Lark's Head Knot

2. Anchor one side of 36-inch strands, leaving half of 36-inch strands and both sides of

132-inch strand to work with (Photo A). At center of 36-inch lines, start making **half-hitch knots** over all strands with one 132-inch strand (*see illustration*) (Photo B).

Half-Hitch Knot

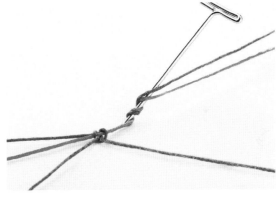

Photo A

Photo B

MATERIALS
80–100 mixed beads
   in shades of brown
   and amber
Large-hole button for
   closure
Waxed linen:
   1 spool light brown,
   1 spool dark brown

11 x 8-inch foam core
   work board
T-pins
Beading glue

FINISHED SIZE
Adjusts from 7¼–8½
   inches (including clasp)

3. Continue making half-hitch knots until you have a section long enough that when it is folded in half it will make a loop that will fit over closure button.

Note: *Knots will want to twist around base strands. For loop section, use fingers to force knots to lay straight. For body of bracelet, allow knots to twist (Photo C).*

Photo C

4. Once it is long enough, un-anchor long strands anchored in step 2. Fold strands over, forming knotted section into a loop. Anchor strand at center of loop. Make two more half-hitch knots over all strands with same short strand (Photo D).

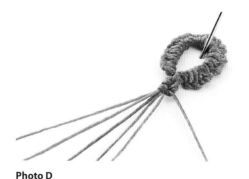

Photo D

5. Continue making half-hitch knots until line used for knotting becomes 3 inches long. Bring knotting line down with rest of base strands and switch to knotting with other side of 132-inch strand, over all other strands, including 3-inch tail. Knot four or five half-hitch knots over base strands. Cut 3-inch tail off at base of knots.

6. Continue making half-hitch knots until bracelet is ½ inch shorter than desired length. Include loop from step 4 in this measurement. **Note:** *If knotting line becomes too short to work with, switch to using one of the 36-inch ends of line in the same manner as step 5.*

7. Slide button over all strands, stopping ½ inch from last knot. Fold all strands over and hold along length of bracelet. Using same line as end of step 6, start knotting half-hitches at base of button over all strands. Continue until knots meet up with knots on bracelet base (Photo E).

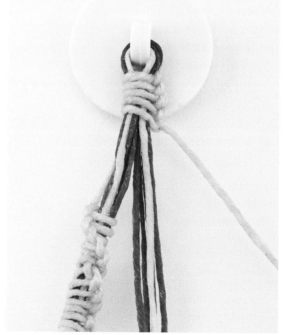

Photo E

8. Brush beading glue over final knots. When glue is dry, trim excess tails.

9. Cut a 3–4-inch strand of light brown waxed linen. Knot strand around center of bracelet using a **square knot** (*see illustration*). String a bead onto one end of strand; tie an **overhand knot** next to bead large enough to hold bead on strand (*see illustration*). Repeat on other side.

Square Knot   Overhand Knot

Note: Small beads can be placed two to a strand before knotting. If there are beads with holes too large to be held on with knot, slide on a seed bead before knotting.

10. Repeat step 9, ½ inch from base of loop and ½ inch from base of button.

11. Continue adding beads up and down bracelet until desired fullness has been reached. To get an even fullness along length of bracelet, start filling in a few ties at a time between first three (Photo F).

Photo F

Note: Beads can be tied so that all fall on same side of bracelet. You can also tie beads so that they fall on all sides of bracelet making it fuller. This method will take up some of the length and will make bracelet fit smaller than with beads all on one side (Photo G). ●

Sources: *Waxed linen from Royalwood Ltd.; mixed beads from Eclectic Etc. Inc.*

Photo G

In the Woods

Combining different shades and shapes of wooden beads keeps this multi-strand set lightweight and easy to wear. When you realize how quickly it goes together, you'll be searching for more ways to use this wonderful design.

Necklace

1) Cut two 15-inch pieces of cotton cord.

2) String jump ring onto one length of cotton cord. Slide jump ring 2 inches down cord, make two **half-hitch knots** to hold the jump ring in place (*see illustration*). Don't trim the end.

Half-Hitch Knot

3) String a copper beaded rondelle and a twist oval brown bead. Repeat pattern until there are fourteen brown beads on cord. Finish with a copper beaded rondelle. Slide the end through another jump ring; make two half-hitch knots snug against the last beaded rondelle.

4) Brush a small amount of beading glue onto the last knot on each end. When the glue is dry, trim the excess cord.

5) Repeat step 2 with the second piece of cotton cord.

6) String a copper double rondelle bead and a black round bead. Repeat pattern until there are fourteen black beads on cord. Finish with double rondelle. Slide end through another jump ring and make two half-hitch knots snug against last double rondelle.

7) Repeat step 4.

8) Cut copper chain in two equal pieces. Use copper jump ring to attach last link of one length of chain to the jump rings on one end of each of the beaded cords. Repeat on other end of the cords with remaining length of chain.

9) Use jump rings to attach the ball and socket clasp to the ends of the chain.

10) Cut five 6-inch pieces of cord.

NECKLACE MATERIALS

Wood beads: 14 (14 x 7mm) brown twist oval, 14 (10mm) black grooved round, 10 (9 x 6mm) brown tube, 10 (4 x 7mm) black rondelles

Copper rondelles: 15double, 25 beaded

10 copper beaded snowflakes

10 inches copper chain
8 copper jump rings
Copper ball-and-socket clasp
60 inches brown cotton cord
Round-nose pliers
2 pairs of chain-nose pliers
Beading glue

FINISHED SIZE
20 inches (including clasp)

11) Make a **lark's head knot** over beaded rondelle at center of cord beaded with brown beads (*see illustration*). On one end of cord slide on a brown tube bead, double rondelle, black rondelle bead and a snowflake. Tie an **overhand knot** at end of cord (*see illustration*). Repeat on the other end of cord. Brush on a small amount of beading glue on end of knots. Trim off any excess cord.

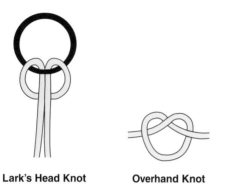

Lark's Head Knot   **Overhand Knot**

12) Repeat step 11 over every third beaded rondelle to each side of the center of beaded cord.

Bracelet

1) Cut 10-inch piece of cotton cord.

2) String jump ring onto cord; slide down 1½ inches. Make two half-hitch knots to hold jump ring in place (*see half-hitch knot illustration on page 57*). Don't trim the end.

3) String a beaded rondelle, oval twist brown bead, beaded rondelle and a black round bead. Repeat four times. Finish with a beaded rondelle, oval twist and a beaded rondelle. Slide end of cord through another jump ring and make two half-hitch knots snug against the last beaded rondelles (*see half-hitch knot illustration on page 57*).

4) Brush a small amount of beading glue onto last knot on each end. When glue is dry, trim the excess cord.

5) Attach ball-and-socket clasp to jump rings on each end of bracelet.

BRACELET MATERIALS
Wood beads: 6 (14 x 7mm) brown twist oval, 5 (10mm) black grooved round, 2 (9 x 6mm) brown tube, 2 (4 x 7mm) black rondelles
Copper rondelles: 2 double, 12 beaded
2 copper beaded snowflakes

2 copper jump rings
Copper ball-and-socket clasp
15 inches brown cotton cord
2 pairs of chain-nose pliers
Beading glue

FINISHED SIZE
8 inches (including clasp)

6) Cut a 5-inch piece of cotton cord. Tie cord in a **square knot** at one end of bracelet between knot and last beaded rondelle (*see illustration*). On one end of the cord string a brown tube bead, double rondelle, black rondelle bead and a snowflake. Tie an overhand knot at the end of cord. Repeat on other end of cord.

Square Knot

7) Brush a small amount of beading glue onto knot on each end. Trim off any excess cord.

Earrings

1) Cut two 4-inch pieces of cotton cord.

2) On one piece string a snowflake bead and fold the cord in half. Over both strands of cord string a black rondelle bead, double rondelle and a brown tube bead.

3) String one tail through a jump ring and make half-hitch knots over both strands of cord down to tube bead (*see half-hitch knot illustration on page 57*). Using other tail make an overhand knot around the center cord next to jump ring (*see overhand knot illustration on page 58*).

4) Brush beading glue onto the end of both knots. When the glue is dry, trim the ends.

5) Attach the jump ring to one ear wire.

6) Repeat for the second earring. ●

EARRINGS MATERIALS
Wood beads: 2 (9 x 6mm) brown tube, 2 (4 x 7mm) black rondelles
2 double copper rondelles
2 copper beaded snowflakes
2 copper jump rings
2 copper French hook ear wires
2 (4-inch) lengths brown cotton cord
2 pairs of chain-nose pliers
Beading glue

FINISHED SIZE
2 inches long

Sources: *Wood beads from Eclectic Etc. Inc.; copper rondelles from Fire Mountain Gems and Beads; chain and cord from Rings & Things; Natural Elegance earwires from Blue Moon Beads; copper jump rings from Rona Horn Designs.*

Harvest Time

This necklace of simple macramé knots between artisan glass beads and resin beads shows how mixing materials and techniques can create a unique handcrafted piece that really stands out. The use of waxed linen and knotting techniques opens up a whole new world of possibilities in your jewelry-making experience.

Project note: *Having necklace anchored while you work helps to make snug, even knots. To anchor your necklace, you can use masking tape to attach piece firmly to a table top, T-pins to pin bracelet to cardboard, foam core or a piece of ceiling tile or a clip board.*

1) Cut waxed linen as follows: one 120-inch length avocado, one 120-inch length gold and one 36-inch length avocado. Hold two 120-inch lengths together; fold in half to find center. Fold 36-inch length in half; make a **lark's head knot** over both long strands at center (*see illustration*).

Lark's Head Knot

2) Using T-pins and foam core board, anchor one side of 120-inch strands, leaving half of 120-inch strands and both sides of 36-inch strands to work with (Photo A). Hold both strands of short avocado together making **half-hitch knots** over two long strands for 1–1½ inches (*see illustration*) (Photo B). **Note:** *The half-hitch knot will*

Half-Hitch Knot

begin to form a twist. Force knot to lay flat with fingers while forming knot (Photo C).

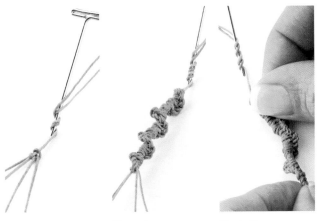

Photo A   Photo B   Photo C

3) Un-anchor long strands anchored in step 2. Fold strands over forming knotted section into loop. Anchor strand at center of loop. Holding both short avocado strands together, knot two or three half-hitch knots over all four strands below knots of loop (Photo D).

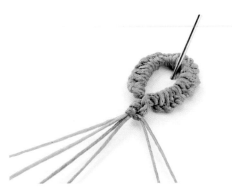

Photo D

MATERIALS

8 (19mm) matte amber resin rondelles
7 (10-12mm) coordinating lampwork spacer beads
12 inches decorative brass chain with open links
Waxed linen: 1 spool gold, 1 spool avocado
2 (7 x 5mm) brass oval jump rings

Antique gold ball-and-socket clasp
Wire flush cutters
11 x 8 foam core board
T-pins
Tapestry needle

FINISHED SIZE

23³⁄₁₆ inches (including clasp)

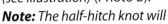

4) Begin making flat knots with short strands of avocado waxed linen. There are two steps to making a flat knot. For **first step of flat knot**, anchor center lines tightly, cross left line over center lines forming a figure four. Bring right line over tail, under center lines, and up trough loop of left line (*see illustration A*). Pull tight. The **second step of a flat knot** is the opposite of first step (*see illustration B*). Cross right line over center lines, forming a backwards figure four. Bring left line over tail of right lines, under center lines, and through loop of right line. Pull tight. Knot in this manner for ¼ inch, keeping count of how many knots are made.

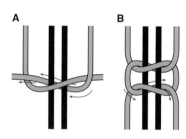

Flat Knot

5) Slide one resin bead over all six strands. Cut off one short length of avocado waxed linen at base of resin bead.

6) Using two strands of gold waxed linen, begin making flat knots. Make same number as in step 4.

7) Slide on one glass spacer bead. Cut off remaining short length of avocado waxed linen at base of glass spacer bead. Using two strands of avocado waxed linen, make another section of flat knots as in step 4.

8) Continue in this manner, alternating resin beads and glass spacer beads and changing waxed linen colors between each bead.

9) After eighth resin bead, make one complete flat knot.

10) Using two strands of gold waxed linen, begin making half-hitch knots skipping about ½ inch of strands with no knots. Using both strands of gold waxed linen, make half-hitch knots over two avocado strands for 1–1½ inches, forming knotted area that will be loop at end of necklace (See note in step 2).

11) Fold knotted section into a loop as in step 3. Make two more half-hitch knots over unknotted area from step 10 and both avocado strands with gold strands. Cut off both avocado strands.

12) Separate two strands of gold waxed linen and begin making flat knots up to resin bead.

13) Using a tapestry needle, tuck gold strands through last resin bead. Cut gold strands on other side of resin bead.

14) Separate brass chain into two equal pieces.

15) Slide one end of one brass chain through one loop of waxed linen, making a loop of chain. Using both pairs of chain-nose pliers, open last link of chain. Connect opened link of chain to second or third link; close chain link. Repeat with second chain on other end of necklace.

16) Using brass jump rings, attach clasp to ends of chain. ●

Sources: *Resin beads from Natural Touch Beads; lampwork glass spacers from Rona Horn Designs; waxed linen from Royalwood Ltd.; brass chain from Funky Hannah's; Lost and Found jump rings from Blue Moon Beads.*

Photo Index

10, Enchanted Forest

13, Forged Fashion

16, Who's Got the Button?

18, Around the Bend

20, Earthy Delight

22, Elemental Metal

24, Be Mused Be Inspired

26, Black Tie Glamour

29, Ocean Waves

32, Romantic Memory

35, Black and White and Bold

38, Drops of Honey

41, Tribal Adornments

44, Wonderful Brass Windows

47, Autumn Medley

50, Woodland Walk

52, Knot Right Now

56, In the Woods

60, Harvest Time

Buyer's Guide

Due to the ever-changing nature of the bead industry, it may be impossible to find the exact beads and components used in the designs shown in this publication. Similar beads may be found via the Internet or by visiting your local bead shops and shows.

AMR GlassWorks
www.amrglassworks.net

Artbeads.com
(866) 715-BEAD (2323)
www.artbeads.com

The Bead Gallery
(716) 836-6775
www.beadgallery.com

The Bead Monkey
(952) 929-4032
www.thebeadmonkey.com

Beadaholique
www.beadaholique.com

Beadalon
(866) 4BEADALON
www.beadalon.com

Beadbury
(763) 425-4520
www.beadbury.com

Beaded Impressions Inc.
(800) 532-8480
www.abeadstore.com

The Beadin' Path
(877) 92-BEADS (922-3237)
www.beadinpath.com

Blue Moon Beads
(800) 727-2727
www.creativityinc.com/
bluemoonbeads

Connie Fox
(888) 350-6481
www.jatayu.com

Darice Inc.
(866) 432-7423
ww.darice.com

Eclectic Etc. Inc.
(888) 746-7382
www.eebeads.com

Fire Mountain Gems and Beads
(800) 423-2319
www.firemountaingems.com

Funky Hannah's
(262) 634-6088
www.funkyhannahs.com

Gail Hughes
(859) 625-9529

Halcraft USA
(914) 840-0505
www.halcraft.com

Hirschberg Schutz & Co.
(908) 810-1111

Jeff Barber
www.lakesideartglass.com

Julie Nordine
www.creditriverartglass.com

Michaels Stores Inc.
(800) MICHAELS (642-4235)
www.michaels.com

Monsterslayer Inc.
(505) 598-5322
www.monsterslayer.com

Natural Touch Beads
(707) 781-0808
www.naturaltouchbeads.com

Ornamentea
(919) 834-6260
www.ornamentea.com

Plaid Enterprises Inc.
(800) 842-4197
www.plaidonline.com

Rings & Things©
(800) 366-2156
www.rings-things.com

Rona Horn Designs
www.ronahorn.com

Royalwood Ltd.
(800) 526-1630
www.royalwoodltd.com

Silk Painting is Fun
(928) 607-2765
www.silkpaintingisfun.com

Soft Flex Co.
(866) 925-3539
www.softflexcompany.com

Thunderbird Supply Co.
(800) 545-7968
www.thunderbirdsupply.com

Tim Holtz
www.timholtz.com

Turtle Island Beads
(608) 356-8823
www.turtleislandbeads.com

The Buyer's Guide listings are provided as a service to our readers and should not be considered an endorsement from this publication.

EDITOR Barb Sprunger

ART DIRECTOR Brad Snow

PUBLISHING SERVICES DIRECTOR Brenda Gallmeyer

ASSISTANT ART DIRECTOR Nick Pierce

COPY EDITORS Emily Carter, Amanda Scheerer

TECHNICAL EDITOR Corene Painter

PHOTOGRAPHY SUPERVISOR Tammy Christian

PHOTO STYLISTS Tammy Leichty, Tammy Steiner

PHOTOGRAPHY Andrew Johnston, Matthew Owen

PRODUCTION ARTIST SUPERVISOR Erin Augsburger

GRAPHIC ARTISTS Glenda Chamberlain, Edith Teegarden

PRODUCTION ASSISTANTS Marj Morgan, Judy Neuenschwander

Annie's Attic®

978-1-59635-307-7

1 2 3 4 5 6 7 8 9